The Rise of Anime and Manga

EXPLORING ANIME

From Pocket Monsters to Jujutsu Sorcerers

MARI BOLTE

TWENTY-FIRST CENTURY BOOKS / MINNEAPOLIS

To all the hours I've spent watching anime—even the fillers

Twenty-First Century Books™
An imprint of Lerner Publishing Group, Inc.
241 First Avenue North
Minneapolis, MN 55401 USA

For reading levels and more information, look up this title at www.lernerbooks.com.

Main body text set in Bembo Std Regular.
Typeface provided by Monotype Typography.

Library of Congress Cataloging-in-Publication Data

Names: Bolte, Mari author
Title: Exploring anime : from pocket monsters to jujutsu sorcerers / Mari Bolte.
Description: Minneapolis, MN : Twenty-First Century Books, 2026. | Series: The rise of anime and manga | Includes bibliographical references and index. | Audience: Ages 11–18 | Audience: Grades 7–9 | Summary: "Many anime are adapted from manga or light novels, but some are completely original! From the sub versus dub debate to anime's global impact, discover more about anime and how it's grown beyond its medium"—Provided by publisher.
Identifiers: LCCN 2025011229 (print) | LCCN 2025011230 (ebook) | ISBN 9798765662731 library binding | ISBN 9798348029630 paperback | ISBN 9798348000363 epub
Subjects: LCSH: Anime (Motion pictures)—Juvenile literature | Anime (Television programs)—Juvenile literature
Classification: LCC NC1766.J3 B64 2026 (print) | LCC NC1766.J3 (ebook) | DDC 791.43/34—dc23/eng/20250519

LC record available at https://lccn.loc.gov/2025011229
LC ebook record available at https://lccn.loc.gov/2025011230

Manufactured in the United States of America
1 – CG – 12/15/25

CONTENTS

INTRODUCTION

In Japan, anime refers to any kind of cartoon or animation. Outside of the country though, people tend to see anime as a Japanese creation. Some people think of anime as epic battles, mecha robot fights, magical girls, or cute talking animals. It can be all of that—and more. Japan has a rich tradition of anime, from its earliest beginnings as silent film to modern, slick animated series.

Anime comes in many genres. There are anime for small children that teach life lessons. There are anime for adults that follow a character's day at work or their dating life. The two most common types, shonen and shojo, are geared toward young viewers but enjoyed by all ages. In Japan, anime is a way of life, with popular characters showing up on food packaging, as statues in public places, and in fine art installations. Even theme parks have been created based on anime. The worlds, characters, and stories have endless creative possibilities.

Almost twenty million people visited Akihabara, Japan, in 2023. Nicknamed "Akiba," the area is famous for its electronics and anime shops.

CHAPTER ONE

The Anime Renaissance

Anime has been around for more than one hundred years. In its early days, it was short and silent. Each slide was drawn by hand. Once it was over, the slides were erased and reused for the next picture. Anime creators not only drew inspiration from traditional Japanese stories but also from tales around the world, overseas studios such as Disney, and even everyday things in their lives.

Around 800 million people outside of Japan and China enjoy anime, and that number is expected to hit one billion by 2027. Between merchandise, theatrical releases, special events, and streaming, anime is a $31 billion industry, with an estimated growth of 10 percent per year from 2024 to 2030. Companies from around the world have noticed. Disney+ launched a streaming hub in 2021 that included access to anime. The hub is called Disney Plus Star and is available in most countries outside the United States. In 2022, Netflix added forty anime titles to their streaming service. The following year, Crunchyroll, the biggest anime streaming service in the world, signed a deal with Amazon

Doraemon receives a large platter of dorayaki, or pancakes filled with sweet bean paste, from Foreign Minister Masahiko Komura.

Video so viewers can subscribe to Crunchyroll directly through Amazon.

Anime characters are even given official positions. In 2008, the robot cat Doraemon, star of one of Japan's most famous manga and anime, was named an anime ambassador. Foreign Minister Masahiko Komura handed Doraemon an official certificate and then presented him with his favorite treat. "Doraemon, I hope you will travel around the world as an anime ambassador to deepen peoples' understanding of Japan so they will become friends with Japan," the foreign minister said. In 2021, a green version of Doraemon was named the Global Sustainability Ambassador for the Japanese clothing company UNIQLO to promote their

Collect 'Em All

Japan's long cultural history is one to be valued, studied, and kept for future generations. In 2015, Japan's Agency for Cultural Affairs unveiled a massive website for keeping records and storing information related to anime and manga. It was called the Media Arts Database. The project began in 2010, and it collects data on manga, manga magazines, video games, and anime. It even holds information on media arts events and exhibits that took place in Japan between 1951 and 2014. In total, there is information on approximately 250,000 manga volumes, 80,000 magazines, 9,000 anime titles, 35,000 games, and 10,000 cultural events. Some of the earliest works date back to the mid- to late-1800s. Future animators and mangaka can find inspiration—and support—from the agency.

message of sustainability. And in 2023, the big blue cat was seen picketing in front of the G7 Summit alongside climate activists. Although this last appearance wasn't officially sanctioned, or approved, the iconic blue-and-white cat's embodiment of peace, friendship, and cooperation fit in well with the message.

An anime's legacy can have an even longer-lasting impact. In 2016, astronomer Edmond Cheung discovered two partner galaxies. He named them Akira and Tetsuo, after characters from Katsuhiro Otomo's anime and manga *Akira*. A new crustacean species was discovered in 2024. It is both male and female. So the scientist who found it named it *Apseudes ranma*, after Rumiko Takahashi's *Ranma ½* character Ranma Saotome, a boy who turns into a girl when splashed with

Akira Toriyama passed away in 2024, but anime fans continue to feel his global impact.

water. In 2018, new dad Carlos Sanchez made a deal with his wife. If he got one million likes on his Facebook post, he would get to name their son Goku, after the main character in Akira Toriyama's *Dragon Ball* series. It happened, and Goku Sanchez was born later that year.

Episode Drops

In Japan, anime episodes are released once a week. This puts the production team on a schedule that allows them time to analyze each episode and fans' reactions to them. Sometimes, fast changes can be made to the episode at the last minute. A weekly schedule keeps fans interested too, as they have to wait another seven days for the next episode. As streaming becomes more popular, services such as Crunchyroll and Hulu make it easy to rewatch episodes during that wait. New fans can also go back and watch missed episodes to catch up. And fans outside of Japan can watch episodes at almost the same time Japanese fans get them.

Some anime, especially those on streaming platforms, drop entire seasons at once. Being able to binge-watch a whole season can provide a lot of hype to get people watching. People wanting to discuss what happened at the end of a season or speculate about what might occur in the next one can stir up interest and make fans happy all at once. Weekly drops and entire-season releases give fans different viewing experiences.

American Pirates

At one point, anime fans in North America had to rely on pirated copies of shows recorded on TVs in Japan. The quality was usually poor, and there were no subtitles. Some shows released videotapes or digital versatile discs (DVDs) with subtitles or even English-language dubs. But they were expensive. Some cost thirty dollars or more and had between one and three episodes. Most stores that carried anime videos had a limited number of volumes and a limited number of series. Being able to watch an entire season could be expensive or even impossible.

In 1997, US cable television channel Cartoon Network began airing Toonami, a block of late-night programming that showed both Japanese anime and American animation. The first anime in the lineup was *Voltron*, an adaptation of several series made by Toei Animation in Japan. *Sailor*

Many traders and collectors buy and collect DVDs online, in stores, and at conventions.

Moon and *Dragon Ball Z* were added shortly after. Since 1998, millions of North American viewers have tuned in to watch anime such as *Attack on Titan*, *The Big O*, *BLEACH*, *Bobobo-bo Bo-bobo*, *Demon Slayer: Kimetsu no Yaiba*, *Sword Art Online*, and *The Prince of Tennis*. Other American-made animation, such as *The Powerpuff Girls*, *Johnny Bravo*, and *Samurai Jack*, got their start on Toonami as well.

Contemporary anime fans have plenty of places to watch their favorite shows. They can stream, download, or buy digital copies and get DVDs and Blu-rays shipped from anywhere in the world. With a few presses of a button, they can change the audio or subtitles from Japanese to English to French to Portuguese and many other languages. They

Crunchyroll is the largest anime streaming service in North America. The company frequently has booths at expos and fan events such as New York Comic Con.

can read series synopses online if they don't want to watch hundreds of back episodes. They can interact with other fans on forums, in online groups, or in person at conventions. Old and new fans can share common favorites, discover new series, and even learn how to make their own anime.

Crunchyroll

Crunchyroll was formed in 2006. But it was not a legitimate company. It was a pirating site where fans could upload and download anything anime-related. The site included original Japanese-language content as well as fan-translated work. People could share their own videos and leave comments. Many other pirating sites existed at the time, but the Crunchyroll founders wanted to build more than a peer-to-peer file sharing service—they wanted to build a culture and a community.

As traction for the site grew, Crunchyroll's founders proved that there was a market for anime. They got investors on board, removed all pirated material, and began offering licensed material only. Subscription plans came later.

Another streaming service, Funimation, partnered with Crunchyroll in 2016. Funimation was acquired by Sony in 2017. The next year, Funimation's content was pulled from Crunchyroll after Sony signed a deal with Hulu. Sony already had its own distribution company, Aniplex, and also owned three other anime distribution companies. In 2019, Sony's distributors were all merged into one.

In 2022, Funimation merged with Crunchyroll. Combined, they had 7.5 million paid subscribers. By January 2024, that number had reached 13 million. In February of that year, however, Crunchyroll announced that the Funimation platform would come to an end in April. The price for Crunchyroll went up from fifty-five to one hundred dollars per year, and digital copies of Funimation Blu-rays and DVDs were no longer supported. It was a disappointment for some longtime fans.

Visit Akihabara

Gamers, otaku, and pop culture nerds alike flock to Akihabara, a famous shopping hub in the center of Tokyo, Japan. Its streets are lined with electronics shops and vending machines for figurines, snacks, toys, and even mystery boxes. Gaming arcades attract both tourists and professional esports players. Theaters draw in popular music groups. People can visit themed cafés and even cosplay as their favorite characters. Many of the stores in Akihabara cater to multilingual customers, advertising that they speak languages including English, Chinese, Korean, Bengali, Russian, and Portuguese. Every year, hundreds of thousands of people from around the world visit "the otaku capital."

One of Akihabara's nicknames is "Electric Town" due to being a major hub for household electronic goods after World War II.

American voice actor Zach Aguilar, who provided the English voiceover for Tanjiro Kamado, poses with his character at the 2023 premiere of *Demon Slayer: Kimetsu no Yaiba—To the Swordsmith Village*.

Despite the hike in price and the lack of service, Crunchyroll accounted for 36 percent of Sony Entertainment's profit in 2024. The company announced that *Demon Slayer: Kimetsu no Yaiba,* the Infinity Castle arc, would be released in a three-part installment in movie theaters. The earlier film installment, *Demon Slayer: Mugen Train*, was the highest-grossing Japanese film in the world. It made more than $500 million at the box office.

CHAPTER TWO

All About Anime

In the 1980s and early 1990s, animation from Japan set itself apart from animation made in the United States and other parts of the world. At one point, all animation from Japan was called "Japanimation," a mix of the words *Japan* and *animation*. People in other parts of the world had been getting familiar with Japanese animation since the 1960s when *Astro Boy* came out. Early anime artists were inspired by Disney's techniques. But over time, they developed their own style. Not all anime has characters with big eyes, simple faces, and dramatic hair—although many do.

Eye See You

Few characteristics of anime are as iconic as a character's big eyes and big hair. Their expressive eyes make it easier for animators to convey emotion, and big, spiky, or colorful hair gives characters a unique look. But anime has a few other features that set it apart from other styles of animation.

Most people in anime are drawn with body types that

Simpler designs often mean that animators can make characters more expressive.

mimic reality. Even if some features are overly emphasized, their muscles still move in a realistic way. Compare that to some American animated characters, such as Fred Flintstone, the Minions, or SpongeBob SquarePants. The latter all have human-like forms, but their heads, arms, and bodies are not drawn with realistic proportions. Interesting camera angles and a character's surroundings and environment add depth to anime as well. American animation tends to have backgrounds that don't move. They're more of a stage for the main characters. Anime backgrounds often have leaves that move, water that flows, and cityscapes full of life.

Drawn This Way

You might not think so, but many popular American cartoons were—and still are—animated overseas, often in Japan, South Korea, and other Asian countries. Some cartoons were even outsourced to Canada or Mexico. Doing this lowered production costs for the studios significantly. It also opened up the job market to people who had the skills but who lived outside the United States. The scripts and voice

Let's Naruto Run Together

The ninja in Masashi Kishimoto's hit series *Naruto* run in a very distinctive style, leaning forward while sweeping their arms back behind them. The run became a meme, a gif, and an inside joke for fans. The run was so iconic, in fact, that a wikiHow page was published in 2008 that explained the technique. In 2014, a stuntman began creating YouTube videos doing parkour while incorporating the run. In Brazil, thousands of people gathered for a real-life Naruto run. An Olympic sprinter even timed himself running normally and doing the Naruto run. (He found that running like a fictional ninja was actually 3 percent slower.)

One of the most famous Naruto runs came in 2019 when a Facebook event called Storm Area 51, They Can't Stop All of Us gained traction as people online claimed they were going to try to take over the infamous classified Air Force facility. One participant saw media cameras and did the Naruto run behind the anchor. The video became a viral sensation. The Naruto run is just one way anime continues to permeate its way into society.

Near the Storm Area 51 event, a music festival called Alienstock took place in Rachel, Nevada. The event featured a Naruto running race for fans of the anime.

work were done in America. Then, outside companies would create the animation.

Japan was doing it too. In the early 2010s, around one-third of Japanese animation was being outsourced. Their workers lived in India, the Philippines, South Korea, and beyond. But no matter where the animation work was being done, the specific cartoon was done in the style that would best fit its market. Japanese anime looked like anime. American cartoons, such as *Thunder Cats*, *The Simpsons*, and *GI Joe*, were drawn to appeal to American viewers. TMS Entertainment is one of the oldest animation studios in Japan. Its parent company is SEGA. It was founded in 1946. TMS

Inspector Gadget was originally planned as a futuristic version of *Lupin III*, called *Lupin VIII*. The project was eventually scrapped and *Inspector Gadget* became its own show.

is behind popular anime such as *Lupin III*, *Bananya*, *Case Closed*, and *Blue Box*, which all share iconic Japanese anime characteristics. But they also animated American cartoons such as *DuckTales*, *Batman: The Animated Series*, *Inspector Gadget*, and *Tiny Toon Adventures* in styles appealing to American audiences at the time.

As anime got more popular outside of Japan, American companies began to take notice. They started making their own shows in an anime-adjacent style. *Avatar: The Last Airbender*, *Samurai Jack*, and *The Powerpuff Girls* all fit that category. And they were all animated in South Korea.

Popularity Comes with a Price

Anime can be expensive to make. Its creation can involve

many costs, including buying the manga rights, developing additional storylines and characters, hiring and recording voice actors, composing and recording music, actual animation work, and more. But it can pay off, especially if the manga has a huge pre-existing fan base that will watch and buy merch for an upcoming anime adaptation.

In 2023, fifty-four new anime premiered during the winter season. Forty-eight were based on manga, video games, and light novels—novels similar to traditional books but with manga-style illustrations. Only six were original series without source material. Because most studios consider original series risky to produce—with little-to-no guarantee that they will make a return on their investment—very few get made each year.

In 2023, *Jujutsu Kaisen* replaced *ONE PIECE* as the most popular manga ever. Its anime, which premiered in 2020, earned a Guinness World Record in 2024 for the world's most in-demand anime series. Global demand for the anime was 71.2 times greater than the average TV show. At its peak, it had 128 times the viewers than the average show. And the cost of the show matches its popularity—with each episode costing around $150,000 to make. But with thirty tankobon volumes of manga as of 2024, as well as tons of official merchandise such as apparel, blind boxes, FUNKO Pop! figurines, and Blu-rays and DVDs, studios have plenty of ways to make their money back. Some figures sell for hundreds of dollars at retail price whereas others are sold to the highest bidder for up to thousands of dollars as collectables. With such a huge following, each piece of merchandise purchased is an advertisement for the rest.

But Where to Start?

Anime can be a quick watch or a huge commitment! Some anime are short. Episodes of Hetalia: Axis Powers are only five minutes apiece. Other anime are long—and have a huge franchise. For example, more than twenty anime series and more than thirty movies have been made for the popular mecha franchise Gundam over the last four and a half decades. Meanwhile, the longest-running anime is Sazae-San, which first appeared in 1969 and is still being made as of 2024. It would take more than fifty-five days to watch every episode back-to-back.

Japan Loves Anime from Anywhere

While most people think of anime as a product of Japan, some shows are created by non-Japanese teams and remain beloved by Japanese watchers. Some of these productions draw on Japanese source material. *Super Mario Bros.* is one example. The video game was published by game developer Nintendo. Hollywood made two *Super Mario Bros.* movies, which came out in 1993 and 2023. *Dr. STONE* is written by Riichiro Inagaki, who is Japanese, but illustrated by Boichi, a South Korean manhwa artist. And *RWBY,* created by Monty Oum—an American of Cambodian, Chinese, Japanese, and Vietnamese descent—and animated by VIZ Media, an American media company, was the top-watched anime on Crunchyroll in Japan between 2010 and 2020. While the numbers are a little skewed since most Japanese people don't use Crunchyroll to watch anime, the fact that it was popular—and that it got a Japanese dub—is significant.

Panda and the Magic Serpent is an adaptation of a Chinese tale called *The Legend of the White Snake.*

Sometimes, anime TV shows get movies. Most are non-canonical and have their own standalone story. They are usually made for the Blu-ray/DVD market, but some get theatrical releases. The first theatrically released anime was *Panda and the Magic Serpent* in 1958. But it wasn't until 1988 that *Akira*, based on an adult manga of the same name, captured moviegoers in Japan, the United States, and beyond. Before *Akira*, the global image of Japan was either that of a feudal society of samurai and swords or a hypermodern marriage between humans and technology. *Akira*, and the anime that followed, showed people outside the country that

The Original Soundtrack

The music used in a show is called the original soundtrack, or OST. This can be background music, opening and ending theme music, diegetic music, and more. Many OSTs are compiled onto a soundtrack album that can be purchased or streamed. One of the most well-known anime composers is Joe Hisaishi, nicknamed the "John Williams of Japan." He has written music for all of Studio Ghibli director Hayao Miyazaki's movies except one. Kohei Tanaka is another well-known anime composer, responsible for the scores of *ONE PIECE*, *Gunbusters*, and *Sakura Wars*.

The opening theme to any show can make it instantly recognizable, even if people aren't familiar with the show itself. *Cowboy Bebop* was picked up by American network executives because its opening sequence, "Tank!" by Yoko Kanno, was so dynamic and catchy. Here are the top ten most-streamed anime opening themes on Spotify in 2024:

1. "Gurenge" by LiSA—*Demon Slayer: Kimetsu no Yaiba*
2. "Kaikai Kitan" by Eve—*Jujutsu Kaisen*
3. "Duvet" by bôa—*Serial Experiments Lain*
4. "KICK BACK" by Kenshi Yonezu—*Chainsaw Man*
5. "Idol" by YOASOBI—*Oshi no Ko*
6. "unravel" by TK from Ling tosite sigure—*Tokyo Ghoul*
7. "The Brave (Yuusha)" by YOASOBI—*Frieren: Beyond Journey's End*
8. "Inferno" by Mrs. GREEN APPLE—*Fire Force*
9. "Silhouette" by KANA-BOON—*Naruto Shippuden*
10. "Shinzo wo Sasageyo!" by Linked Horizon—*Attack on Titan*

Japan was just like other places—full of regular people with regular relationships, problems, and dreams.

Boom to Bust to Rebirth

Japan's economy made huge strides between the end of World War II and the late 1980s, becoming the second-largest economy in the world. Japanese businesses set up offices in the United States and other Western countries. People became more interested in learning the country's culture and its language. The internet made it easier for them to expand their interests. To young people at the time, Japan seemed like a thrilling place of futuristic cyberpunk technology. They might not be able to fly there, but they could get a slice of Japanese life through its media. As anime became more mainstream and fandoms became more dedicated, studios began to take notice. The first two *Pokémon* movies did well, grossing nearly $86 million and $45 million, respectively. The TV series went on to air in 177 countries.

In the 1990s, the bubble of prosperity burst, and Japan was desperate to find ways to regain their lost money and status. Instead of exporting cars and electronics, it turned to something it had a lot of—culture. Video games, manga, anime, food, and other unique pieces of Japanese culture were exported and shared with the world. By 2001, filmmaker Hayao Miyazaki had entranced the world with *Spirited Away*. It held the title of Japan's highest-grossing film of all time for nineteen years. And anime has only continued to grow. Its popularity has been compared to rock 'n' roll and Hollywood movies.

CHAPTER THREE

The Voices of Anime

A single anime might have dozens of different characters, and each character needs a unique voice to go with it. *Astro Boy* was released dubbed in English in 1963, just months after the show premiered in Japan. Its success led to more English-language dubs, including dubs for *Tetsujin 28-go* (*Gigantor* in English), *Kimba the White Lion*, and *Speed Racer.* In 1988, Streamline Pictures was founded with the intent to produce and distribute anime to English-speaking countries. It was the first company of its kind.

In Japan, voice actors are called *seiyu.* They do voiceover work for anime, video games, commercials, and other things that may need dubbing. The professional magazine *Seiyu Grand Prix* began tracking how many seiyu were working in 2001. That year, there were 225 actresses and 145 actors. By 2023, there were 1,030 actresses and 655 actors. Some of the most well-known seiyu today include Natsuki Hanae, who has worked on shows such as *Demon Slayer: Kimetsu no Yaiba*, *Tokyo Ghoul*, *Stars Align*, and *Tsukimichi: Moonlit Fantasy*; Rie Takahashi, who has worked on shows such as *Seiyu's Life!*,

Natsuki Hanae has been voice acting since 2011.

Re:Zero—Starting Life in Another World, and *Rent-a-Girlfriend*; and Takehito Koyasu, who has voiced characters in *Neon Genesis Evangelion*, *JoJo's Bizarre Adventure*, and *Shaman King*, among many others. In 2024, Koyasu was the Guinness World Record holder for most prolific male anime voice actor.

There are fewer anime voice actors in the United States. In the 1990s, when anime was still finding its place, voice actor Marin Miller quipped that the entire dubbing industry was "basically the same ten people." Many actors at the time weren't familiar with dubbing or skilled in matching their words with existing animation. As anime grew, more actors entered the industry. Funimation founded its first studio for dubbing anime in 1994. For more than a decade, it was small and poorly funded. This inexperience from all sides led to actors being exploited. Being overworked, underpaid, and ignored have been complaints among voice actors for decades. As animation companies grew, they had even more power, especially over new actors.

Shouting On- and Off-Screen

In 2016, video game voice actors went on strike with the help of the Screen Actors Guild – American Federation of Television and Radio Artists (SAG-AFTRA), the largest entertainment and media industry union in the world. The strike lasted for more than a year, leading to bigger payouts and more transparency from production companies about how budgets were being spent. After the strike, the Coalition of Dubbing Actors (CODA) formed to help unite voice actors. Together, CODA and SAG-AFTRA helped increase hourly rates and obtained greater bargaining power for workers. But there are still issues. Voice acting seems like it would be a high-paying career. Online, you can find popular actors' net worth to be in the millions. But the reality is often the opposite. "I've never seen a million dollars in my life," Ben Diskin, a voice actor for more than three decades, said after seeing his worth estimated at around five million dollars. "We're thousand-aires, at best. . . . Most just live paycheck to paycheck."

To drive the point home, the 2021 movie *Jujutsu Kaisen*

In the summer of 2024, video game voice actors went on strike against employers to demand protection against artificial intelligence.

0 earned more than $30 million in the United States alone. Some of the English-language voice actors report they were paid as little as $150 for their work. Many supplement their incomes by making appearances at anime conventions. Diskin points out that this transfers the responsibility of paying actors for their roles from the studios to the fans.

Meet the Cast

Some well-known English-language voice actors include Wendee Lee, who has supplied the voice in shows such as *Dragon Ball, Fushigi Yugi*, and *Blue Exorcist*; Veronica Taylor, who voiced Ash Ketchum in *Pokémon* and appeared in other anime including *Dragon Ball Super* and *Sailor Moon Crystal*; and Christopher Sabat, who lent his voice to characters in shows such as *The New Prince of Tennis*, *Fullmetal Alchemist*, and *Black Butler.*

Sometimes, anime gets even more highbrow by enlisting A-list Hollywood actors. In 1996, Disney acquired worldwide distribution rights to Studio Ghibli movies. They redubbed all the films using well-known Hollywood actors. Patrick Stewart, Christian Bale, Daisy Ridley, and Dakota Fanning are only a few famous actors who lent their talent to Hayao Miyazaki's works. Other well-known stars who love anime and became part of the cast include Samuel L. Jackson (*Afro Samurai*), John Cho (*Mirai*), and Emily Rudd (*Delicious in Dungeon*).

Read-Alongs

Although it is common for anime to have dubs, every show needs closed-captioning. This practice originates in the United States, where text appears along the bottom of the screen to allow deaf or hard of hearing people to follow along by reading. In Japan, any superimposed text is called *telop*. When that text is translated, it's called subtitles, or "subs" for short. Today, subtitles in multiple languages are standard in film and TV around the world.

It takes talent to translate subtitles that match the context of the characters. Subtitles offer a little more freedom since the words on the screen don't have to match the characters' mouth movements. But there is limited space on-screen, and not all phrases or expressions translate easily. If the subtitles are too wordy, people might not be able to keep up, or they may get bored. But offering quality subtitles has helped anime find success with viewers in foreign countries who don't mind reading along.

Well-known actors Robert Pattinson, Florence Pugh, Dave Bautista, and Mark Hamill provided the English voiceovers for some of the main characters in *The Boy and the Heron*.

CHAPTER FOUR

Anime Overseas

Anime has changed the way many people appreciate and understand cartoons. Instead of viewing them as funny, lighthearted, or juvenile productions aimed at children, many people learned that themes such as anger, sadness, or power could be brought to life through animation. For example, emotionally charged animated films such as *Big Hero 6*, *Turning Red*, and *Lilo & Stitch* all draw from Japanese movies and culture—especially Studio Ghibli movies. The 2024 DreamWorks movie *The Wild Robot* was directly inspired by Miyazaki's movie *Castle in the Sky*. *How to Train Your Dragon* spun the human-dragon relationship by adding a Miyazaki-inspired vulnerability in both Hiccup and Toothless. Dean DeBlois, the movie's director, said that the thing that sets anime apart is its bravery in storytelling. It doesn't get hung up in what the market wants or what will sell. "There's no overthinking of who the audience is," he said. "It's just about what would be spectacular, what would be emotional, and what would really be resonant."

By the end of 2024, *The Wild Robot* had grossed more than $324 million worldwide and was nominated for an Academy Award for Best Animated Feature Film.

Getting Serious

In anime, sometimes characters die. They cry. They grieve. Anime is not afraid to tackle heavy subjects. In the past, many American cartoons have skirted these issues, but bigger story arcs and deeper character development have become more commonplace within the last two decades. Steven Universe, Avatar: The Last Airbender, Gravity Falls, and She-Ra and the

Princesses of Power don't shy away from redemption, loss, and love. And they've paved the way for animation that can handle even heavier topics. By 2023, the demand for animation for adults had jumped more than 150 percent over three years.

Streaming is one of the main ways people watch anime around the world, but there are problems figuring out just how popular it really is. For one, not every streaming company offers every show. It's also hard to know exactly who is watching, since families or households tend to share accounts. In 2024, Netflix reported that anime watching in the second half of 2023 had reached 3.5 billion hours, or nearly 4 percent of all viewership. When measured against the metric gathered in the first half of the year, that meant anime watchers had added an extra three weeks of viewing from July to December. The streaming company went into the next year with big hopes, releasing Dungeon Meshi, or Delicious in Dungeon in English, in January. The show would become the streamer's most-watched anime in the first half of the year, followed by Demon Slayer, Spy x Family, and Jujutsu Kaisen.

Anime in Arabic

In the 1970s and 1980s, Arabic-dubbed anime came to the Middle East. It was a hit. "The streets in Jordan would be empty when [anime was] on," actor Mohammed Ramadan remembers. "As soon as it finished, we'd go out to play and imitate the martial arts moves we'd seen in *Grendizer* [*UFO Robot Grendizer* in English] or the football moves from *Captain Majid* [*Captain Tsubasa* in English]." The same shows were on every day at the same time. Watching TV after school and on the weekend was a custom all kids at this time

In 2017, Saudi Comic Con became Saudi Arabia's first pop culture convention. It was a government-sponsored event designed to bring more entertainment to the country.

participated in.

Saudi Arabia and Japan have a decades-long history of cooperation, exchanging both oil and culture to further their countries. The Gulf Cooperation Council Joint Program Production Institution was founded in 1976 with the intent of creating, translating, and dubbing manga and anime in the Middle East. They distributed familiar stories such as *The Adventures of Sinbad* to get people re-interested in Arabic

Qiddiya City is an entertainment district that includes twelve theme parks, a performing arts center, areas devoted to gaming and esports, and themed hotels.

and Islamic history. And, like American TV producers, they adapted foreign shows such as *Sesame Street* and *Dragon Ball Z* to fit their viewers' culture and values.

In 2017, three hundred animators from Saudi Arabia's Manga Productions were sent to Japan to learn how to make anime at Toei Animation. Both Japanese and Saudi animators noticed similarities between their cultures—such as a desire for order, a belief in scientific advancement, and persevering

through challenges. The resulting movie, called *The Journey*, was released in 2021. In 2023, Saudi Arabia invested heavily in Toei Animation, and the following year, work on the very first *Dragon Ball Z* theme park began in Qiddiya City in Riyadh, Saudi Arabia.

CHAPTER FIVE

Live-Action Anime

Anime fans can experience their favorite shows both on- and off-screen. Stage play adaptations of anime, also known as 2.5D musicals, let audiences get up close and personal. These adaptations include original songs, impressive fights, choreographed dances, and, of course, special themed merchandise that draw in music and anime fans alike.

The first successful manga-based 2.5D musical was an adaptation of Riyoko Ikeda's *The Rose of Versailles* in 1974, but the first anime-based performance would not get one until 2003. More than two million theatergoers flocked to see a live performance of Takeshi Konomi's *The Prince of Tennis* in Japan that year. Since then, hundreds of adaptations have been created and performed. In 2024, *ATTACK on TITAN: The Musical* played in New York City. It was directed by a breakdance world champion. Supertitles were projected above the stage for non-Japanese speakers. Unusually enough, the *Death Note* musical, which premiered in 2015, was written in English, not Japanese. Its composer, lyricist, and scriptwriter were all white Americans.

An all-female theater troupe, Takarazuka Revue, performed the first 2.5D musical for *The Rose of Versailles*.

Many anime also get live-action film or TV adaptations. Some fans feel that live-action productions never live up to their expectations. After all, it can be hard—or even impossible—to portray some of anime's most fun or interesting effects. Other times, the live action strays too far from the original source material, alienating longtime fans and confusing potential new ones. There have been some successes though. *Nana*, *Death Note*, *The Ingenuity of the Househusband*, *Jojo's Bizarre Adventure*, *Kimi ni Todoke*, and *Cutie Honey* are a few generally well-regarded adaptations.

The main cast of Netflix's live-action ***ONE PIECE*** adaptation meet fans at a global fan event ahead of season one's premiere in summer 2023.

In the United States, *Alita: Battle Angel*, *Detective Pikachu*, and *Cowboy Bebop* are some other examples of live-action anime fans generally enjoy. Netflix's 2023 adaptation of *ONE PIECE* was particularly well received. The first season was the most-watched Netflix series in eighty-four countries, with 18.5 million streams its first week.

Cosplays and Cons

People who dress up in costumes as their favorite fictional anime, TV, video game, or manga characters are called cosplayers. Designing and building the most authentic costumes and accessories possible is often the goal. Fans might take their cosplays to conventions or other events. Within the United States alone, there are hundreds of anime conventions. Some of the biggest are Anime Expo, Anime Matsuri, and San Diego Comic-Con. These conventions give cosplayers opportunities to meet their favorite authors, illustrators, or voice actors in person, as well as buy merchandise unique to their interests. Cosplayers can even join contests at these conventions where judges determine the best cosplay. These contests are often divided into categories for novices, intermediates, and masters. Some even have a performance category where cosplayers can dance and act.

Fans and cosplayers recreate Goku's signature move, the Kamehameha, from *Dragon Ball*.

CHAPTER SIX

Bringing Fans Together

Anime can get inspiration from anywhere. Stories can come from historical events, mythological tales, or events in the author's own life. Anime can also be based on books, light novels, manga, or even video games. Some actually got their start as video games!

Pokémon is one of the more well-known video games that later became an anime. The franchise began as the role-playing games *Pokémon Red* and *Green*. The games were released for Nintendo Game Boy in 1996. North American versions, *Pokémon Red* and *Blue*, were released two years later. As of 2024, there were thirty-four core games across nine console generations. And the franchise's legacy continues on. Every February 27, to commemorate the original Japanese release date of the first games, people around the world celebrate Pokémon Day and wait for announcements about the newest Pokémon releases.

The Pokémon Trading Card Game was created and sold in Japan in 1996. The game came to the United States three years later. Huge tournaments pitted the best players in the

There are more than two hundred thousand unique Pokémon cards.

world against each other. Others collected the cards to simply enjoy them. In March 2022, an Illustrator Pikachu card sold for $5,275,000. YouTube influencer Logan Paul was the highest bidder. It became the most expensive Pokémon card ever sold.

Manga creator Hidenori Kusaka was chosen to turn *Pokémon* into manga. *Pokémon Adventures* came out in 1997 and has run continuously for more than two decades and covers the entire video game franchise history. There are twenty-five main characters across the series.

For a long period of time, a *Pokémon* game and movie were released every year. The COVID-19 pandemic in 2020 interrupted this streak.

The *Pokémon* anime series aired in Japan in 1997 and worldwide the next year. (It was released in North America twenty days before *Pokémon Red* and *Blue* came out.) Japanese kids watched Satoshi—named after the franchise's creator, Satoshi Tajiri—collect cuddly creatures and battle with gym leaders. Americans knew him as Ash Ketchum. By 2024, more than one thousand episodes across twenty-three seasons had been made. As of 2023, there were also twenty-eight total movies, and each of them starred Ash.

Living History

Anime museums exist all over Japan. The Suginami Animation Museum in Suginami City, Japan, is surrounded by more than seventy animation studios. Visitors can see how a series is made from start to finish. A large collection of items belonging to famous writers is on display at the museum. People can also visit its large library of anime.

The Toei Animation Museum opened in Nerima, Japan, in 2018 and is free. The company's history stretches more than six decades of popular shows and movies. There are life-size statues, vending machines, and interactive exhibits.

The Ghibli Museum in Mitaka, Japan, was designed by Hayao Miyazaki himself. A theater shows short films and video clips, and rotating exhibits present drawings, scripts, layouts, and other pieces of history. Visitors are free to explore, relax, and enjoy the museum at their own pace.

A Totoro statue, from the film *My Neighbor Totoro*, greets visitors at the Ghibli Museum.

Gathering as a Group

Pokémon isn't the only anime franchise that has a huge fan following. In 2023, hundreds of *Demon Slayer* fans gathered in Times Square in New York City. Cosplayers dressed as their favorite characters. Crunchyroll employees handed out T-shirts. One group of friends even brought a cake. They weren't there for a convention though. There wasn't a star-studded appearance or even a 2.5D performance going on that night. The show's season finale was coming up.

At nine o'clock p.m., everyone turned their attention to the huge TV screens around them. A two-minute promo video teasing the final episode played. When the words "SEASON FINALE TOMORROW. BINGE IT ALL."

Nani?

In 2023, the language learning app Duolingo teamed up with Crunchyroll. Japanese is one the top four most-requested languages to learn in the United States, along with Spanish, French, and English, and as anime grows, so do the number of fans who want to watch in its native language. Around 26 percent of Duolingo Japanese learners reported that wanting to watch anime in Japanese was their main motivation to learn. Duolingo offered a special course with nearly fifty phrases from popular anime. Duo the Owl also recommended his top ten favorite anime series of all time. This list included *Nichijou: My Ordinary Life, Hyouka, My Hero Academia*, and *New Game!* There was also a short list of series with fairly basic vocabulary that learners could watch and learn from.

Duolingo has more than 500 million registered users interested in learning more than forty different languages.

appeared on the screen, the fans went wild. For the next hour, the video replayed on a loop, and the gathered crowd stayed to rewatch it, chat, and discuss what they might see the following night.

Watch and Learn

Anime can bring people together. It can also be used as a teaching tool. Some anime are based on historical events, involve real people, or are set during actual periods in history. *Black Butler*, *Emma*, and *Moriarty the Patriot* are all set in the Victorian era. They depict social classes, architecture, and Victorian tropes such as rags-to-riches stories or contrived coincidences. *InuYasha* takes place during Japan's Sengoku Jidai period (1467–1615), *Samurai Champloo* falls in the Edo period (1603–1868), and *Demon Slayer* happens during the Taisho era (1912–1926).

Some anime have an educational aspect, although being a teaching tool isn't its primary point. Sports anime, including *Haikyu!!, Yuri!!! on Ice, The Prince of Tennis, Free! – Iwatobi Swim Club*, and *Blue Box*, tell compelling stories that happen to take place around games, matches, or competitions. *Seiyu's Life!, SHIROBAKO*, and *Girlish Number* give a behind-the-scenes look at how anime and manga are created and the work that goes into them. *The Magnificent Kotobuki, Vinland Saga*, and *Grave of the Fireflies* give audiences a peek at historical events and invite them to learn more after watching. Artists pay close attention to details of airplanes, ships, and buildings, which add to the authenticity of the story.

Anime can also be used as a direct teaching tool wherein

Demon Slayer is one of the most-watched anime since it first aired in 2019.

The 1954 tokusatsu film *Godzilla* has grown into a worldwide franchise. In 2024, Godzilla got a new look with the fully animated *Godzilla x Kong: The New Empire*.

students take on a more active role in their learning. Rather than students sitting passively learning the same thing through lectures, teachers can connect with their students through shows. It's not only educational, it's fun too!

Cells at Work! is an example of an anime that mixes imagination with education. It takes place inside a human body, and the characters are all cells that look like people. The main characters are a red blood cell and a white blood cell. They do tasks for their "job"—for example, the red blood cell brings oxygen to organs in the human body, and the white blood cell fights off infections that take on the form of a classic "monster of the week"—to help the human body function. *The Heroic Legend of Arslan* tells the story of a Persian prince fighting a war. Maps, military strategy, and mythology combine to tell a compelling story based on real-life history. *Jaku-Chara Tomozaki-Kun* (*Bottom-Tier Character Tomozaki*) is about a gamer who wants to learn life and social skills.

Anime's Cousin

The word *tokusatsu* means "special effects." It refers to live-action movies and TV shows that center around special effects. Because it has many of the heroic, dramatic, and flashier elements associated with anime, people consider tokusatsu to be "anime's cousin." The most famous example of tokusatsu is kaiju movies such as *Godzilla* or *King Kong*. *Kamen Rider* was a tokusatsu based on a manga and was later turned into an anime as well. *Super Sentai*—or *Power Rangers* in North America—is another well-known tokusatsu series.

Tokusatsu anime is not as common. The special effects that look realistic and fun don't translate as well to animation. There are also plenty of live-action and 2.5D versions already out there. But there are tokusatsu anime being made. *Go! Go! Loser Ranger!* and *The Red Ranger Becomes an Adventurer in Another World* are two examples that embrace spandex costumes and masks alongside special effects tropes.

Cashing In

Anime fans love anime no matter where they are—among friends, at school, and even at home. In 2023, fans spent more than $5.4 billion on merchandise. That's expected to reach nearly $9.4 billion per year by 2030. That's billions of dollars spent on figurines, T-shirts, phone accessories, trading cards, and more. Fans also buy mobile games, tokusatsu merchandise, and J-pop albums from artists who specialize in anime theme music. In 2024, the best-selling anime series was *Demon Slayer*. *Ensemble Stars* and *My Hero Academia* were

The animate Ikebukuro Flagship Store hosts fan events such as movie screenings, autograph signings, performances, and pop-ups.

the runners-up.

Little kids are no longer the largest target market for licensed products from their favorite shows. Instead, adults eighteen and over—referred to as "kidults"—have taken over the toy industry, spending the most on anime merchandise for themselves. To meet this demand, the animate Ikebukuro Flagship Store opened in Tokyo, Japan, in 2023 in a former health center. It was nine floors and two basement levels full of licensed anime, manga, video games, music, and more. In 2024, Guinness World Records named it the largest anime store in the world.

And it's not just Japanese or American fans buying everything anime-related. Anime-wear is huge in places such as India. Market visitors to Delhi can choose from multiple stalls overflowing with anime shirts. Pratik Purohit, an advertising professional, wasn't afraid to share his thoughts on style. "I love buying anime-themed T-shirts," he said. "I feel wearing an anime tee of my favorite character is more than a style statement. It serves as motivation as it reminds me of the anime character's journey." In Africa, brands such as La Lunary and Isekai South Africa design and sell anime clothing and cosplay items. Festivals give fans a unique opportunity to purchase limited-time or exclusive merch as well. The Èkó Anime Fest is held in Nigeria. It was first held in 2022 and grows every year. Otamatsuri takes place across the continent in Kenya. Its name comes from *otaku* and *matsuri*, which means "festival" in Japanese.

CONCLUSION

Cue the Outro

The anime market continues to grow by leaps and bounds. People around the world of any age, gender, or interests enjoy watching and talking about anime. They don't even need to speak Japanese! Anime gives viewers a way to escape reality and inspires their imaginations to create their own. Thanks to streaming, they can binge-watch anime anywhere they go and can meet other fans at conventions or online. They can find shows with hundreds of episodes or watch a ninety-minute movie. Anime covers war, grief, happiness, friendship, magic, love, and anything in between. If it can be imagined, an anime about it probably exists.

Japan isn't the only country making and exporting anime, and its creators are both sources of inspiration and taking inspiration from others. Its influence is felt in the United States, South America, the Middle East, and beyond. As technology moves forward, anime will move with it.

Anime fans can attend one of thousands of cosplay events across North America. Some events are small local gatherings, while others are huge well-known conventions in major US and Canadian cities.

GLOSSARY

adaptation: a written work that has been reworked to be a movie, TV show, or play

ambassador: a person who acts as a representative of an activity or a country

arc: the continuing plot of a novel or a story with a clear beginning, middle, and end

cable television: a system of television programming delivered to consumers through coaxial or fiber-optic cables

canon: a work of fiction that is either created by or officially approved by the original author or developer of the world

console: an electronic device that plays a video game

cosplay: dressing up as a character from a movie, show, book, or video game

cyberpunk: a genre of science fiction that combines lawless society and futuristic technology

diegetic: sounds or music that exists inside a story's fictional world that both the character and the audience can hear, such as music on a radio or performances within the show

digital versatile disc (DVD): a type of compact disc that can store large amounts of data

ending theme: music that plays at the end of a movie, TV show, or radio program

fandom: the fans of a particular person, fictional series, or team

franchise: a series of books, TV shows, or movies that have the same or similar names and are about the same characters or the same universe

genre: a style of a creative work

gross: the amount of money something earns before taxes and expenses are taken out

kaiju: a giant monster found in Japanese fantasy and science fiction works

LGBTQIA+: short for *lesbian, gay, bisexual, transgender, queer or questioning, interesex, asexual or aromatic*, and *others*

manhwa: a South Korean genre of comic books, graphic novels, and webtoons

mecha: a large, armored robot, usually controlled by a person inside

opening theme: music that plays at the beginning of a movie, TV show, or radio program

otaku: a person very interested in anime, manga, video games, or computers

pirate: a person who takes or copies someone else's work for profit and without permission

prosperity: the condition of being successful or thriving

streaming: a method of sending or receiving data over a computer network in a continuous flow

sustainability: the ability to be maintained at a certain rate or level

synopsis: a brief summary

trope: an overused theme or device

union: a group of employees who join together for a common cause, such as fair working hours or pay

SOURCE NOTES

7 "Doraemon, I hope . . . friends with Japan.": Masahiko Komura, quoted in Blake Hounshell, "Japan Appoints Anime Ambassador," *Foreign Policy*, March 19, 2008, https://foreignpolicy.com/2008/03/19/japan-appoints-anime-ambassador/.

27 "basically the same ten people": Marin Miller, quoted in Rohan Montgomery, "Anime Voice Actors Speak Out: It's Not Kawaii When We Aren't Paid," *In These Times*, February 20, 2023, https://inthesetimes.com/article/anime-dubbing-voice-actors-union-crunchyroll-funication-jjk-aot-coda.

28 "I've never seen . . . paycheck to paycheck.": Ben Diskin, quoted in Rohan Montgomery, "Anime Voice Actors Speak Out: It's Not Kawaii When We Aren't Paid," *In These Times*, February 20, 2023, https://inthesetimes.com/article/anime-dubbing-voice-actors-union-crunchyroll-funication-jjk-aot-coda.

32 "There's no overthinking . . . really be resonant.": Dean DeBlois, quoted in Evan Henerson, "The Influence of Anime," *Keyframe Magazine*, August 14, 2020, https://keyframemagazine.org/2020/08/14/the-influence-of-anime/.

34 "The streets in . . . from Captain Majid.": Muhammed Ramadan, quoted in Indlieb Farazi Saber, "Why Anime Has Such Deep Roots in the Arab World," *Middle East Eye*, August 10, 2021, https://www.middleeasteye.net/discover/anime-arab-world-popularity-middle-east.

53 "I love buying . . . anime character's journey.": Pratik Purohit, quoted in Shivika Manchanda, "Otakus Say Anime T-Shirts are More than a Style Statement," *Times of India*, April 6, 2024, https://timesofindia.indiatimes.com/life-style/spotlight/otakus-say-anime-t-shirts-are-more-than-a-style-statement/articleshow/109082585.cms.

SELECTED BIBLIOGRAPHY

Brzeski, Patrick. "How Japanese Anime Became the World's Most Bankable Genre." *The Hollywood Reporter*, May 16, 2022. https://www.hollywoodreporter.com/business/business-news/japanese-anime-worlds-most-bankable-genre-1235146810/.

MediaTech. "Anime's Pressure on American Animation." MediaTech, August 14, 2023. https://mediatech.edu/animes-pressure-on-american-animation/.

Nickerson, Andrew. "History: How Anime Can Teach It Better Than Our Schools." Anime Herald, October 8, 2021. https://www.animeherald.com/2021/10/08/history-how-anime-can-teach-it-better-than-our-schools/.

Polygon Staff. "Anime Is Huge—And Here Are the Numbers to Prove It." Polygon, January 22, 2024. https://www.polygon.com/c/2024/1/22/24034466/anime-viewer-survey-research.

Rich. "How I Learned to Stop Worrying and Love Being Otaku: Answering Questions of Identity and Fandom in Japan and Beyond." *Tofugu*, June 6, 2016. https://www.tofugu.com/japan/otaku-meaning/.

FURTHER INFORMATION

Books

Alt, Matt. *Pure Invention: How Japan's Pop Culture Conquered the World*. New York: Crown, 2020.
Read the untold story of how Japan became a pop culture superpower.

Bond, Jeff, and Gene Kozicki. *Cowboy Bebop: Making the Netflix Series*. London: Titan Books, 2022.
This is an official guide showing readers how the transition from *Cowboy Bebop*'s anime to live action took place.

Gossin, Pamela. *Cultural Guide to Anime and Manga*. San Diego: ReferencePoint Press, 2024.
Dive deep into anime and manga and how they have infused people's lives.

Kallen, Stuart A. *Exploring Animation*. San Diego: ReferencePoint Press, 2025.
Follow the path of animation from concept art to computer-generated films.

Mooney, Carla. *World of Anime*. San Diego: BrightPoint Press, 2024.
Explore some of the most popular anime, its history, and the important people who made it what it is today.

Sattin, Samuel, and Patrick Macias. *A Kid's Guide to Anime & Manga: Exploring the History of Japanese Animation and Comics*. Philadelphia: RP Kids, 2023.
This is an accessible, inclusive guide for young fans who love anime.

Websites

Britannica: Anime
https://www.britannica.com/art/anime-Japanese-animation
This site gives the history, summary, and importance of anime in Japan and around the world.

Comic Book Resources: Anime
https://www.cbr.com/tag/anime/
Learn more about what anime is, why people like it, and recommendations to watch.

EAC Library
https://eac.libguides.com/c.php?g=723550&p=5215189
Here is a timeline of the history of anime, complete with screenshots and video clips.

Japan Craft: What Is the Difference Between Manga and Anime?
https://japancraft.co.uk/blog/manga-anime-difference/
This helpful blog summarizes manga and anime and offers additional information about Japanese culture.

Japan Powered: What Makes Anime, Anime?
https://www.japanpowered.com/anime-articles/what-makes-anime-anime
Enjoy a breakdown, complete with screenshots, of common themes that identify anime.

Nashville Film Institute: What is Anime? Everything You Need to Know
https://www.nfi.edu/what-is-anime/
Explore everything you need to know about anime.

INDEX

ABOUT THE AUTHOR

Mari Bolte is a Korean-American writer and editor who lives in Minnesota with her family and a zoo of pets. She loves books in all formats, but has a special fondness for manhwa and manga.

PHOTO ACKNOWLEDGMENTS

Image credits: visualspace/Getty Images, p. 5; Junko Kimura/Getty Images, p. 7; Fotoholica Press/Getty Images, p. 9; asiangrandkid/Shutterstock, p. 11; Craig Barritt/Getty Images, p. 12; Pola Damonte via Getty Images/Getty Images, p. 14; JEAN-BAPTISTE LACROIX/Getty Images, p. 15; Stefano Chiacchiarini '74/Shutterstock, p. 17; BRIDGET BENNETT/Getty Images, p. 19; Album/Oronoz/Newscom, p. 20; LMPC/Getty Images, p. 23; Craig Barritt/Getty Images, p. 27; VALERIE MACON/Getty Images, p. 29; ULIL TRAPSILA/Shutterstock, p. 31; Shane Anthony Sinclair/Getty Images, p. 33; FAYEZ NURELDINE/Getty Images, p. 35; FAYEZ NURELDINE/Getty Images, p. 36; TOSHIFUMI KITAMURA/Getty Images, p. 39; Alexandre Schneider/Getty Images, p. 40; Daniel Knighton/Getty Images, p. 41; Robert vt Hoenderdaal/Getty Images, p. 43; John Hanson Pye/Shutterstock, p. 44; cowardlion/Shutterstock, p. 45; PixieMe/Shutterstock, p. 47; Usa-Pyon/Shutterstock, p. 49; John Springer Collection/Getty Images, p. 50; SOPA Images/Getty Images, p. 52; picture alliance/Getty Images, p. 55.

Cover image: yopinco/Getty Images